Pumped

Great Words to Keep You Going When Hope Is Hard To Come By

Mary Pat Boland

Dedication

This book is dedicated to the memory of three people: My parents, Raym and Mary Boland. Mum taught me to love words through good books and reading. Dad taught me through his wonderful Irish blarney. Doctor T. taught me ... everything.

Acknowledgements

There are so many people who have encouraged me through the years, and I thank them all. Several deserve special recognition: my aunt and my friend, Jean Kull, and my niece and nephews, Lucas Boland, Jarrad Caola, and Jessie Caola Cohodar.

I thank four wonderful friends who served as my personal editors: Anna Wyche, Barbara Shane, Cheryl Satterthwaite, and Devra Boesch. I deeply appreciate the time and effort they spent in reading the manuscript and offering me their *many* corrections and suggestions. (I especially appreciate Anna pointing out to me that I have not yet mastered the English alphabet.) Any improvements to this book are due to their advice, lovingly offered.

Thanks, also, to Mickey Cuzzucoli for suggesting the title and for pushing me to Get. It. Done.

Very special thanks to Nick Galifianakis of the *Washington Post* who allowed me to use his drawing for my cover page. It perfectly conveys what I feel on finally seeing this volume to completion: *Yes!* To see more of Nick's wonderful work, check out his website at http://nickandzuzu.com.

Table of Contents

Introduction

I have been saving quotes since my college days. Sometimes I review my collection with a specific goal in mind, for example, to improve a paper I am writing. Sometimes I look at it to fill the quiet hours. This volume was put together specifically for those who are job hunting or who will be making the big presentation which has the potential to change their lives.

Although there are countless quotations which could have been included, I deliberately chose to limit the number in order to keep the finished book small. I want it to be portable. I hope you, the reader, will mark it up and dog-ear it, carry it with you, and refer back to it often. Let it provide you with inspiration, encouragement right before you walk through that potentially life-changing door, and if need be, let it bring you comfort and the will to keep trying when the people behind that door say *no*.

In addition to the quotes, this book also includes short passages on people who have been rejected once and have gone on to achieve phenomenal success or those who have been rejected over and over again, but who have persisted and gone on to achieve significant, though not necessarily world-renown, success in their fields. Let their examples provide you with the hope that you, too, can change your life if only you keep trying.

The quotes I have included come from my personal collection as well as many other wonderful (and not so wonderful) sources. I chose them because they illustrate in a few words what most of us would find difficult to express in many. Although some are short, I have avoided the trite – no bumper stickers allowed. I looked for words which have stood and will continue to stand the test of time. Through the years, many of the quotes within these pages have helped me when I have gone through my own challenging times. I hope they help you, too.

#

In a few cases where multiple people uttered similar sounding phrases, I chose to include the more poetic of the two, not the one first spoken.

Some compilers of books of quotations have expressed the view that quotes must be linked to a specific person or they are lifeless. I disagree. While it is better to know who said what, I believe wisdom can still be obtained even if we do not know who first uttered the words or in what context, so within these pages you will find a few quotes attributed to Anonymous.

Every effort has been made to acknowledge the author of the quotations used. If any reader of this book can attribute the *anonymous* quotes to a source, or if there are errors in attribution, please contact the editor.

Great Words

Be who God meant you to be, and you will set the world on fire.
Saint Catherine of Siena

Failure is a part of success. There is no such thing as a bed of roses all your life. But failure will never stand in the way of success if you learn from it.
Hank Aaron

I've never doubted my ability, but when you hear all your life you're inferior, it makes you wonder if the other guys have something you've never seen before. If they do, I'm still looking for it.
Hank Aaron

#

Baseball great **Hank Aaron** ended his career as the all-time home-run champion with 3,771 hits. He had 755 home runs and set Major League records for total bases, extra-base hits, and runs batted in. He was the 1957 National League most valuable player and won three Gold Gloves. His beginnings were not so auspicious. The first time he was at bat with the Milwaukee Braves…he went 0 for 5.

#

May your trails be crooked, winding, lonesome, dangerous, leading to the most amazing view. May your mountains rise into and above the clouds.
Edward Abbey

Patience and perseverance have a magical effect before which difficulties disappear and obstacles vanish.
John Quincy Adams

The most sacred place dwells within our heart, where dreams are born and secrets sleep, a mystical refuge of darkness and light, fear and conquest, adventure and discovery, challenge and transformation. Our heart speaks for our soul every moment while we are alive. Listen... as the whispering beat repeats: be...gin, be...gin, be...gin. It's really that simple. Just begin... again.
Royce Addington

Far away there in the sunshine are my highest aspirations. I may not reach them, but I can look up and see their beauty, believe in them, and try to follow them.

Louisa May Alcott

Be brave enough to live creatively. The creative is the place where no one else has ever been. You have to leave the city of your comfort and go into the wilderness of your intuition. You cannot get there by bus, only by hard work, risking, and by not quite knowing what you are doing. What you will discover will be wonderful: yourself.

Alan Alda

Great things are only possible with outrageous requests.

Thea Alexander

Often the test of courage is not to die but to live.

Vittorio Alfieri

Champions aren't made in the gyms. Champions are made from something they have deep inside them – a desire, a dream, a vision.

Muhammad Ali

I hated every minute of training, but I said, 'Don't quit. Suffer now, and live the rest of your life as a champion.'

Muhammad Ali

Each of us has been put on earth with the ability to do something well. We cheat ourselves and the world if we don't use that ability as best we can.

George Allen

Health, happiness and success depend upon the fighting spirit of each person. The big thing is not what happens to us in life, but what we do about what happens to us.

George Allen

Never place a period where God has placed a comma.

Gracie Allen

Eighty percent of success is showing up.

Woody Allen

To play it safe is not to play.

Robert Altman

People will always try to knock you in life – and knock your dreams. In a peculiar way, that's not a bad thing. In the end, it gives you an opportunity to prove you want it enough, and that you're strong enough to keep going.

Christiane Amanpour

Dare to be what you are and learn to resign with a good grace all that you are not and to believe in your own individuality.

Henri-Frédéric Amiel

Work while you have the light. You are responsible for the talent that has been entrusted to you.

Henri-Frédéric Amiel

You can tell how big a person is by what it takes to discourage him.

Amish proverb

I cannot get rid of the hurt from losing, but after the last out of every loss, I must accept that there will be a tomorrow. In fact, it's more than there'll be a tomorrow, it's that I want there to be a tomorrow. That's the big difference. I want tomorrow to come.

George Lee ("Sparky") Anderson

Some people regard discipline as a chore. For me, it is a kind of order that sets me free to fly.

Julie Andrews

Bad news is just additional information.

Anonymous

I didn't know it was impossible when I did it.

Anonymous

I doubt anyone will ever see – anywhere – a memorial to a pessimist.

Anonymous

If Columbus had turned back, no one would have blamed him. Of course, no one would have remembered him either.

Anonymous

In life you will come to great chasms. Leap.

Anonymous

It is probable that many things will happen contrary to probability.

Anonymous

Know your goals: to do, to have, to be. Review them every day. Say them out loud.

Anonymous

Not knowing what to do makes every act possible.

Anonymous

Remember that not getting what you want may be the best thing that never happened to you.

Anonymous

Remember you only need three things. You need great faith. You need great doubt. You need great determination.

Anonymous

What you don't know, somebody else is getting paid for.

Anonymous

When you lose, don't lose the lesson.

Anonymous

Three failures denote uncommon strength. A weakling has not enough grit to fail thrice.

Minna Thomas Antrim
At the Sign of the Golden Calf

I have heard it said that the first ingredient of success – the earliest spark in the dreaming youth – is this: dream a great dream.

John Alan Appleman

He who has health has hope, and he who has hope has everything.

Arab Proverb

There is fear in every hope, and hope in every fear.

Arab Proverb

The wise learn many things from their foes.

Aristophanes
Birds

If you think you can, you can. And if you think you can't, you're right.

Mary Kay Ash

When you reach an obstacle, turn it into an opportunity. You have the choice. You can overcome and be a winner, or you can allow it to overcome you and be a loser. The choice is yours and yours alone. Refuse to throw in the towel. Go that extra mile that failures refuse to travel. It is far better to be exhausted from success than to be rested from failure.

Mary Kay Ash

There is no such thing as *can't*, only *won't*. If you're qualified, all it takes is a burning desire to accomplish, to make a change. Go forward, go backward. Whatever it takes! But you can't blame other people or society in general. It all comes from your mind.

Jan Ashford

It takes little talent to see clearly what lies under one's nose; a good deal of it is to know in which direction to point that organ.

W.H. Auden

Motivation will almost always beat mere talent.

Norman R. Augustine

Patience is the companion of wisdom.

Saint Augustine
On Patience

What can be hoped for which is not believed?

Saint Augustine

A man's happiness is to do a man's true work.

Marcus Aurelius
Meditations

At daybreak, when loath to rise, have this thought in thy mind: I am rising for a man's work.

Marcus Aurelius
Meditations

Genius, that power which dazzles mortal eyes, is often perseverance in disguise.

Henry Willard Austin

I am not a has-been. I am a will-be.

Lauren Bacall

Imagination is the highest kite one can fly.

Lauren Bacall

There's no disaster that can't become a blessing, and no blessing that can't become a disaster.

Richard Bach

What the caterpillar calls the end of the world, the master calls a butterfly.

Richard Bach

Eighteen publishers turned down **Richard Bach**'s manuscript for *Jonathan Livingston Seagull* before Macmillan finally accepted it. When the book was published, it reached the top of the New York Times Best Seller list and was made into a movie. Since 1970, it has sold about forty million copies in at least forty-seven languages.

A wise man will make more opportunities than he finds.

Francis Bacon

They are ill discoverers that think there is no land, when they can see nothing but sea.

Francis Bacon

We must be willing to fall flat on our faces. Fearlessly putting ourselves out there is simply a required part of the process. At the very least, it results in the gift of humility and, at best, the triumph of our human spirit.

Jill Badonsky

You don't get to choose how you're going to die. Or when. You can decide how you're going to live now.

Joan Baez

The real essence of work is concentrated energy.

Walter Bagehot
Biographical Studies

When fortune knocks, be sure to open the door.

Nathaniel Bailey
Etymological Dictionary

It matters not how long we live, but how.

Philip James Bailey
"Festus"

First comes the sweat. Then comes the beauty – if you're very lucky and have said your prayers.

George Balanchine

If you don't live the only life you have, you won't live some other life; you won't live any life at all.

James Baldwin

I don't know anything about luck. I've never banked on it, and I'm afraid of people who do. Luck to me is something else: hard work and realizing what is opportunity and what isn't.

Lucille Ball

I think knowing what you can not do is more important than knowing what you can do.

Lucille Ball

An unfulfilled vocation drains the color from a man's entire existence.

Honoré de Balzac
La Maison Nucingen

There is no such thing as a great talent without great will-power.

Honoré de Balzac
La Muse du Département

The man who can drive himself further once the effort gets painful is the man who will win.

Roger Bannister

Through the night of doubt and sorrow,
Onward goes the pilgrim band,
Singing songs of expectation,
Marching to the Promised Land.

Sabine Baring-Gould

Before you give up hope, turn back and read the attacks that were made on Lincoln.

Bruce Barton

Nothing splendid has ever been achieved except by those who dared believe that something inside them was superior to circumstance.

Bruce Barton

I have an almost complete disregard of precedent, and a faith in the possibility of something better. It irritates me to be told how things have always been done. I defy the tyranny of precedent.

Clara Barton

In 1962, Decca Records turned down **The Beatles**. The company thought that guitar bands were on their way out; instead, they signed up a group called Brian Poole and the Tremolos. In August 2011 - better late than never - Decca announced that it is collaborating with McCartney to release the score of *Ocean's Kingdom*, his first ballet.

Anne Beattie was doing graduate work in English at the University of Connecticut when frustration with her dissertation made her put it aside to work on short stories. She was rejected by *The New Yorker* twenty-two times before they published "A Platonic Relationship" in 1974. Since then, she has published seven novels and seven short story collections. She has won the Award in Literature from The American Academy of Arts and Letters, a Guggenheim Fellowship, and the PEN/Malamud Award for Excellence in Short Fiction.

I really do think that any deep crisis is an opportunity to make your life extraordinary in some way.

Martha Beck

Fail. Fail again. Fail better.

Samuel Beckett

If there were dreams to sell
What would you buy?

Thomas Lovell Beddoes
"Dream-Pedlary"

In the ordinary business of life, industry can do anything which genius can do, and very many things which it cannot.

Henry Ward Beech
Proverbs from Plymouth Pulpit

When one door closes another door opens, but we so often look so long and so regretfully upon the closed door that we do not see the ones which open for us.

Alexander Graham Bell

Those of us who speak out are moved by a deep sense of the fragility of our self-worth. It is the determination to protect our sense of who we are that leads us to risk criticism, alienation, and serious loss while most others similarly harmed, remain silent.

Derrick Bell

If opportunity doesn't knock, build a door.

Milton Berle

It ain't over till it's over.

Yogi Berra

If you don't know where you're going, you will wind up somewhere else.

Yogi Berra

Faith is the substance of things hoped for, the evidence of things not seen.

The Bible
Hebrews 11:1

I have fought a good fight, I have finished my course, I have kept the faith.

The Bible
II Timothy 4:7

To every thing there is a season, and a time to every purpose under the heaven.

The Bible
Ecclesiastes 3:1

A winner is someone who recognizes his God-given talents, works his tail off to develop them into skills, and uses these skills to accomplish his goals.

Larry Bird

I've got a theory that if you give one-hundred percent all of the time, somehow things will work out in the end. Push yourself again and again. Don't give an inch until the final buzzer sounds.

Larry Bird

No bird soars too high if he soars with his own wings.

William Blake

Nothing is predestined. The obstacles of your past can become the gateways that lead to new beginnings.

Ralph Blum

Success is outliving your failures.

Erma Bombeck

There are people who put their dreams in a little box and say, "Yes, I've got dreams, of course, I've got dreams." Then they put the box away and bring it out once in awhile to look in it, and yep, they're still there. These are *great* dreams, but they never even get out of the box. It takes an uncommon amount of guts to put your dreams on the line, to hold them up and say, "How good or how bad am I?" That's where courage comes in.

Erma Bombeck

When I stand before God at the end of my life, I would hope that I would not have a single bit of talent left and could say, 'I used everything you gave me.'

Erma Bombeck

A leader is a dealer in hope.

Napoleon Bonaparte

When all else is lost, the future still remains.

Christian Nestell Bovee

Don't go to the grave with life unused.

Bobby Bowden

At the end of life, when we must all lay ourselves out, with what thoughts shall we do so? Will we think, "I did my best!" or will we think, "I never tried…"

Ray Bradbury

Sometimes you've got to jump off cliffs and grow wings on the way down.

Ray Bradbury

Show me a guy who's afraid to look bad, and I'll show you a guy you can beat every time.

Lou Brock

I believe in personal movement, that movement of the soul when a man who looks at himself is so ashamed that he tries to make some sort of change – within himself, not on the outside.

Joseph Brodsky

No coward soul is mine,
No trembler in the world's storm-troubled sphere:
I see Heaven's glories shine,
And faith shine equal, arming me from fear.

Emily Brontë

You have no idea how promising the world begins to look once you have decided to have it all for yourself. And how much healthier your decisions are once they become entirely selfish.

Anita Brookner
Hotel du Lac

Do not pray for easy lives. Pray to be stronger men. Do not pray for tasks equal to your powers. Pray for powers equal to your tasks. Then the doing of your work shall be no miracle, but you shall be the miracle.

Bishop Phillips Brooks

I do not pray for a lighter load, but for a stronger back.

Bishop Phillips Brooks

An individual's self-concept is the core of his personality. It affects every aspect of human behavior: the ability to learn, the capacity to grow and change, the choice of friends, mates and careers. It is no exaggeration to say that a strong, positive self-image is the best possible preparation for success in life.

Joyce Brothers, Ph.D.

...the only thing that separates successful people from the ones who aren't is the willingness to work very, very hard.

Helen Gurley Brown

Be bold and courageous. When you look back on your life, you'll regret the things you didn't do more than the ones you did.

H. Jackson Brown, Jr.

Never deprive someone of hope; it might be all they have.

H. Jackson Brown, Jr.

Accept responsibility for your life. Know that it is you who will get you where you want to go, no one else.

Les Brown

Shoot for the moon. Even if you miss it, you will land among the stars.

Les Brown

Creativity comes from trust. Trust your instincts. And never hope more than you work.

Rita Mae Brown
Starting from Scratch

Light tomorrow with today.

Elizabeth Barrett Browning

Ah, but a man's reach should exceed his grasp,
Or what's Heaven for?

Robert Browning

The price of victory is high, but so are the rewards.

Paul ("Bear") Bryant

There is no substitute for guts.

Paul ("Bear") Bryant

You never know how a horse will pull until you hook him up to a heavy load.

Paul ("Bear") Bryant

Destiny is not a matter of chance, but a matter of choice. It is not a thing to be waited for; it is a thing to be achieved.

William Jennings Bryant

When the student is ready, the master appears.

Buddhist Proverb

No passion so effectually robs the mind of all its powers of acting and reasoning as fear.

Edmund Burke

I believe that whatever degree of talent I possess is a gift and must be treated as such. To misuse one's talent, to be cavalier about it, to set it aside because of fear or sloth is unpardonable.

James Lee Burke

#

James Lee Burke had already published five books, so it should have been easy to have his manuscript for *The Lost Get-Back Boogie* accepted. But it wasn't. It was rejected 111 times over a period of nine years. [The book holds the distinction of being the most rejected book in New York's publishing history.] It was finally accepted by the Louisiana State University Press – and promptly nominated for a Pulitzer Prize. Since that time, Burke has written twenty-six more books. He's won the Mystery Writers of America's Edgar Awards three times, including the Grand Master Award, the pinnacle of achievement in mystery writing, and two of his books have been made into motion pictures.

#

Make no little plans. They have no magic to stir men's blood. Make big plans: aim high in hope and work.

Daniel Hudson Burnham

Aim for success, not perfection. Never give up your right to be wrong, because then you will lose the ability to learn new things and move forward with your life.

David M. Burns

Dare to be honest and fear no labor.

Robert Burns

Leap, and the net will appear.

John Burroughs

The most painful thing to experience is not defeat but regret.

Leo Buscaglia

A belief may be larger than a fact.

Vannevar Bush
Science Is Not Enough

Optimism is the foundation of courage.

Nicholas Murray Butler

If we attend continually and promptly to the little that we can do, we shall ere long be surprised to find how little remains that we cannot do.

Samuel Butler
Notebooks

Too many people are thinking of security instead of opportunity. They seem more afraid of life than death.
James F. Byrnes

The first step toward success is taken when you refuse to be a captive of the environment in which you first find yourself.
Mark Caine

A leader must have the courage to act against an expert's advice.

James Callaghan

Opportunities to find deeper powers within ourselves come when life seems most challenging.

Joseph Campbell

Where you stumble, there your treasure lies.

Joseph Campbell

Every new opinion, at its starting, is precisely in a minority of one. In one man's head alone, there it dwells as yet. One man alone of the whole world believes it; there is one man against all men.

Thomas Carlyle
On Heroes and Hero Worship and the Heroic in History

Most of the important things in the world have been accomplished by people who have kept on trying when there seemed to be no hope at all.

Dale Carnegie

When we have accepted the worst, we have nothing more to lose. And that automatically means we have everything to gain.

Dale Carnegie

Why, sometimes I've believed as many as six impossible things before breakfast.

Lewis Carroll
Through the Looking Glass

People create their own luck by the choices they make.

Benjamin S. Carson, M.D.

You must accept that you might fail; then, if you do your best and still don't win, at least you can be satisfied that you've tried. If you don't accept failure as a possibility, you don't set high goals, you don't branch out, you don't try – you don't take the risk.

Rosalynn Carter

Where there is great love, there are always miracles.

Willa Cather

Wise men profit more from fools than fools from wise men, for the wise men shun the mistakes of fools, but fools do not imitate the successes of the wise.

Cato the Elder

Crises refine life. In them you discover what you are.

Allen K. Chalmers

Success is often achieved by those who don't know that failure is inevitable.

Gabrielle ("Coco") Chanel

Anton Chekhov's play *The Seagull* was so poorly received when it was first performed in 1896 that the actors were nearly hissed off the stage. Chekhov left the auditorium during the second act and vowed never to write for the stage again. (Luckily for us, he relented.) Over one hundred years later, *The Seagull* is still available for sales in bookstores and still regularly performed on stages throughout the world.

If you want to know your past, look into your present conditions. If you want to know your future, look into your present actions.

Chinese Proverb

Talk doesn't cook rice.

Chinese Proverb

As long as we're caught up in always looking for certainty and happiness, rather than honoring the taste and smell and quality of exactly what is happening, as long as we're always running from discomfort, we're going to be caught in a cycle of unhappiness and discomfort, and we will feel weaker and weaker. This way of seeing helps us develop inner strength. And what's especially encouraging is the view that inner strength is available to us at just the moment when we think that we've hit the bottom, when things are at their worst.

Pema Chodron

Nothing ever goes away until it has taught us what we need to know.

Pema Chodron

The secret of getting ahead is getting started.

Dame Agatha Christie

Acquire the courage to believe in yourself.

Ching Ning Chu

Never, never, never give up.

Sir Winston Churchill

Success is not final, failure is not fatal: it is the courage to continue that counts.

Sir Winston Churchill

The pessimist sees difficulty in every opportunity. The optimist sees the opportunity in every difficulty.

Sir Winston Churchill

Man is a creature of hope and invention, both of which belie the idea that things cannot be changed.

Tom Clancy

We find comfort among those who agree with us, growth among those who don't.

Frank A. Clark

The only way of finding the limits of the possible is by going beyond them into the impossible.

Arthur C. Clarke

Faith is the daring of the soul to go farther than it can see.
William Newton Clarke

Great opportunity is usually disguised as unsolvable problems.
Gretchen G. Clement

If you do not hope, you will not find what is beyond your hopes.
Saint Clement of Alexandria
Stromateis

The past is history, not destiny.
William Jefferson Clinton

Luck is what you have left over after you give one-hundred percent.
Langston Coleman

You will do foolish things, but do them with enthusiasm.
(Sidonie-Gabrielle) Colette

It's amazing how much can be accomplished if no one cares about who gets the credit.
Blanton Collier

Vision: It reaches beyond the thing that is into the conception of what can be. Imagination gives you the picture. Vision gives you the impulse to make the picture your own.
Robert Collier

Perfect freedom is reserved for the man who lives by his own work, and in that work does what he wants to do.
R. G. Collingwood

Choose a job you love, and you will never have to work a day in your life.
Confucius

Wherever you go, go with all your heart.
Confucius

Nothing in the world can take the place of persistence. Talent will not; nothing is more common than unsuccessful men with talent. Genius will not; unrewarded genius is almost a proverb. Education will not; the world is full of educated derelicts. Persistence and determination alone are omnipotent.
Calvin Coolidge

Optimism doesn't wait on facts. It deals with prospects. Pessimism is a waste of time.
Norman Cousins

The tragedy of life is not death, but what we let die inside us while we live.
Norman Cousins

Wisdom consists of the anticipation of consequences.

Norman Cousins

Work is much more fun than fun.

Sir Noël Coward

Knowledge is proud that he has learned so much / Wisdom is humble that he knows no more.

William Cowper
"The Task"

It's not enough to be good if you have the ability to be better. It is not enough to be very good if you have the ability to be great.

Alberta Lee Cox

It took English crime novelist **John Creasey** fourteen years and 753 rejection slips before he finally sold the tenth novel he completed, *Seven Times Seven*. From then on, there was no stopping him. Writing under his own name or one of his numerous pen names, he published 564 books in at least twenty-eight languages with total estimated sales over eighty million copies.

Ten percent is what life brings to you. Ninety percent is what you do about it.

Alice Crowe

Any time you try to win everything, you must be willing to lose everything.

Larry Csonka

To be nobody but yourself - in a world, which is doing its best, night and day, to make you, everybody else - means to fight the hardest battle which any human being can fight; and never stop fighting.

E. E. Cummings

By 1935, **E.E. Cummings** had published five volumes of poetry, a play, and a novel. He had written articles for *Vanity Fair* and *The Dial*. His paintings and drawings had been exhibited. Notwithstanding all that, fourteen publishers refused to publish his most-recent collection of poems. In the end, it was his mother who gave Cummings the money to have the book self-published. Cummings famously un-dedicated the book (appropriately entitled *No Thanks*) - in the form of a funeral urn – to the fourteen publishers which had rejected his manuscript.

NO
THANKS TO
TO
Farrar & Rinehart
Simon & Schuster
Coward–McCann
Limited Editions
Harcourt, Brace
Random -House
Equinox Press
Smith & Haas
Viking Press
Knopf
Dutton
Harper's
Scribner'ss
Covici-Friede

#

Advances are made by those with at least a touch of irrational confidence in what they can do.

Joan L. Curcio

Courageous risks are life giving, they help you grow, make you brave and better than you think you are.

Joan L. Curcio

Jump into the middle of things, get your hands dirty, fall flat on your face, and then reach for the stars.

Joan L. Curcio

The bold are always lucky.

Danish Proverb

Obstacles cannot crush me. Every obstacle yields to stern resolve. He who is fixed to a star does not change his mind.
Leonardo da Vinci

To decide, to be at the level of choice, is to take responsibility for your life and to be in control of your life.

Abbie M. Dale

New York Times bestselling author **Diane Mott Davidson** wrote three novels before one was accepted for publication - when she was forty-one. She has since written fourteen additional mysteries plus short stories and poetry. She has won the Anthony Award from Bouchercon, and has been nominated for the Agatha and the Macavity awards. In 1993, she was named Rocky Mountain Fiction Writers' Writer of the Year.

To fulfill a dream, to be allowed to sweat over lonely labor, to be given a chance to create, is the meat and potatoes of life. The money is the gravy.

Bette Davis

Patience is the art of hoping.

Luc de Clapiers, Marquis de Vauvenargues
Réflexions ou Sentences et Maximes Morales

Out of difficulties grow miracles.

Jean de La Bruyere

They never achieve anything who do not believe in success.

Fernando de Lesseps

No trumpets sound when the important decisions of our life are made. Destiny is made known silently.

Agnes George de Mille
Dance to the Piper

A rock pile ceases to be a rock pile the moment a single man contemplates it, bearing within him the image of a cathedral.

Antoine de Saint-Exupéry

It is only with the heart that one can see rightly; what is essential is invisible to the eye.

Antoine de Saint-Exupéry
The Little Prince

Jesu, good above all others, gentle child of gentle mother, in a stable born our brother, give us grace to persevere.

Percy Dearmer

The world has improved mostly because unorthodox people did unorthodox things. Not surprisingly, they had the courage and daring to think they could make a difference.

Ruby Dee

Know thyself.

Inscription on the Temple to Apollo at Delphi

Small opportunities are often the beginning of great enterprises.

Demosthenes

Sources don't agree on the number – some say ten, some say fifteen, others claim nineteen – but whatever the actual figure, **Patrick Dennis** (born Edward Everett Tanner III) had a hard time getting his manuscript for *Auntie Mame* published. Vanguard Press finally accepted it. [As André Bernard points out in his book, *Rotten Rejections*, that is "...rather deep into the alphabet."] The first edition of the book was on the New York Times bestseller list for 112 weeks and sold more than 2,000,000 copies in five different languages. The novel has been adapted for the stage and turned into a Hollywood film (both starred Rosalind Russell), then re-adapted into a musical for the stage with that version also made into a movie.

To gain that which is worth having, it may be necessary to lose everything.

Bernadette Devlin

Yesterday I dared to struggle. Today I dare to win.

Bernadette Devlin

If I had to select one quality, one personal characteristic that I regard as being most highly correlated with success, whatever the field, I would pick the trait of persistence. Determination. The will to endure to the end, to get knocked down seventy times and get up off the floor saying, "Here comes number seventy-one!"

Richard M. DeVos

Hope is the thing with feathers
that perches in the soul,
and sings the tune--without the words,
And never stops at all.

Emily Dickinson

I dwell in possibility.

Emily Dickinson

The willingness to accept responsibility for one's own life is the source from which self-respect springs.

Joan Didion

Difficult times have helped me to understand better than before how infinitely rich and beautiful life is in every way, and that so many things that one goes worrying about are of no importance whatsoever.

Isak Dinesen

It's kind of fun doing the impossible.

Walt Disney

Action may not always bring happiness, but there is no happiness without action.

Benjamin Disraeli

Patience is a necessary ingredient of genius.

Benjamin Disraeli

Success is the child of audacity.

Benjamin Disraeli

Before you can win, you have to believe you are worthy.

Mike Ditka

I don't think anything is unrealistic if you believe you can do it.

Mike Ditka

Success is never permanent, and failure is never final.

Mike Ditka

Only one thing matters, one thing: to be able to dare!

Feodor Dostoyevsky
Crime and Punishment

The creative individual not only respects the irrational in himself, but counts it as the most promising source of novelty in his own thought.

John H. Douglas

It is an old maxim of mine that when you have excluded the impossible, whatever remains, however improbable, must be the truth.

Arthur Conan Doyle

When nothing is sure, everything is possible.

Margaret Drabble

Happy the man, and happy he alone,
He who can call today his own:
He who, secure within, can say,
Tomorrow do thy worst, for I have lived today.

John Dryden

For a long time it had seemed to me that life was about to begin-real life. But there was always some obstacle in the way, something to be gotten through first, some unfinished business, time still to be served, a debt to be paid. Then life would begin. At last it dawned on me that these obstacles were my life.

Alfred D'Souza

The distance doesn't matter; it is only the first step that is difficult.

Marquise du Deffand (Marie de Vichy-Chamrond)

In knowing how to overcome little things, a centimeter at a time, gradually when bigger things come, you're prepared.

Katherine Dunham

Courage is the price that life exacts for granting peace.

Amelia Earhart

Hold on to your ideals. Sometimes it is important to lose for things that matter.

Marian Wright Edelman

Be courageous, have faith, go forward.

Thomas Edison

If we did the things we are capable of doing, we would literally astound ourselves.

Thomas Edison

I have not failed. I've just found ten thousand ways that won't work.

Thomas Edison

If at first the idea is not absurd, then there is no hope for it.

Albert Einstein

Imagination is more important than knowledge.

Albert Einstein

In the middle of difficult lies opportunity.

Albert Einstein

It is never too late to be what you might have been.

George Eliot (Mary Ann Evans)

Success is relative. It is what we can make of the mess we have made of things.

T.S. Eliot

Do not go where the path may lead, go instead where there is no path and leave a trail.

Ralph Waldo Emerson

Nothing is beneath you if it is in the direction of your life.

Ralph Waldo Emerson

When it is dark enough, you can see the stars.

Ralph Waldo Emerson

He who makes no mistakes never makes anything.

English Proverb

Knowledge is power.

English Proverb

Ask not that events should happen as you will, but let your will be that events should happen as they do, and you shall have peace.

Epictetus

Success seems to be largely a matter of hanging on after others have let go.

William Feather

It's not what you achieve in life, it's what you overcome.

Carlton Fisk

Never confuse a single defeat with a final defeat.
F. Scott Fitzgerald

The test of a first-rate intelligence is the ability to hold two opposed ideas in mind at the same time and still retain the ability to function. One should, for example, be able to see that things are hopeless and yet be determined to make them otherwise.
F. Scott Fitzgerald

... no one who shows courage can be considered a failure.
Penelope Fitzgerald

Don't give up before the miracle happens.
Fannie Flagg
I Still Dream about You

There's a saying among prospectors: Go out looking for one thing, and that's all you'll ever find.
Robert Flaherty

My centre is giving way; my right is in retreat. Situation excellent. I shall attack.
Ferdinand Foch

None but a coward dares to boast that he has never known fear.
Marshal Foch

Genius is seldom recognized for what it is: a great capacity for hard work.
Henry Ford

Life is a series of experiences, each one of which makes us bigger, even though it is hard to realize this. For the world was built to develop character, and we must learn that the setbacks and griefs which we endure help us in our marching forward.
Henry Ford

Obstacles are those frightful things we see when we take our eyes off our goal.
Henry Ford

Take risks, look for gaps, and do what no one else is doing.
Michael J. Fox

To accomplish great things, we must not only act, but also dream, not only plan, but also believe.

Anatole France

Have patience with all things, but chiefly have patience with yourself. Do not lose courage in considering your own imperfections, but instantly set about remedying them. Every day, begin the task anew.

Saint Francis de Sales

Start by doing what's necessary, then what's possible, and suddenly you are doing the impossible.

Saint Francis of Assisi

What man actually needs is not a tensionless state but rather the striving and struggling for some goal worthy of him. What he needs is not the discharge of tension at any cost, but the call of a potential meaning waiting to be fulfilled by him.

Viktor Frankl

Diligence is the mother of good luck, and God gives all things to industry. Then plough deep while sluggards sleep, and you shall have corn to sell and to keep.

Benjamin Franklin

Fear is a question. What are you afraid of and why? Our fears are a treasure house of self-knowledge if we explore them.

Marilyn French

It's all very well in practice, but it will never work in theory.

French Management Saying

God works in moments.

French Proverb

Miracles happen only to those who believe in them.

French Proverb

Necessity is half a reason.

French Proverb

… in the small matters trust the mind, in the large ones the heart…

Sigmund Freud

Now, boys, we have got her done. Let's start her up and see why she doesn't work.

John Fritz

The psychic task, which a person can and must set for himself, is not to feel secure, but to be able to tolerate insecurity.

Erich Fromm

Two roads diverged in a wood, and I,
I took the one less traveled by,
And that has made all the difference

Robert Frost
"The Road Not Taken"

Never forget that you are one of a kind. Never forget that if there weren't any need for you in all your uniqueness to be on this earth, you wouldn't be here in the first place. And never forget, no matter how overwhelming life's challenges and problems seem to be, that one person can make a difference in the world. In fact, it is always because of one person that all the changes in the world come about. So be that person.

R. Buckminster Fuller

A wise man turns chance into good fortune.

Thomas Fuller

Great hopes make great men.

Thomas Fuller

When our hopes break, let our patience hold.

Thomas Fuller

Gold medals aren't really made of gold. They're made of sweat, determination, and a hard-to-find alloy called guts.

Dan Gable

Most of my major disappointments have turned out to be blessings in disguise. So whenever anything bad does happen to me, I kind of sit back and feel, well, if I give this enough time, it'll turn out that this was good, so I shan't worry about it too much.

William Gaines

The difference between what we do and what we are capable of doing would suffice to solve most of the world's problems.

Mahatma (Mohandas) Gandhi

We must become the change we seek.

Mahatma (Mohandas) Gandhi

Your beliefs become your thoughts. Your thoughts become your words. Your words become your actions. Your actions become your habits. Your habits become your values. Your values become your destiny.

Mahatma (Mohandas) Gandhi

If you want a decision, go to the point of danger.

General James M. Gavin

Depending on which version of the story **Theodor Geisel** told, either twenty, twenty-six, twenty-seven, twenty-eight, or twenty-nine publishers rejected his first book for children, *To Think That I Saw It on Mulberry Street.* Then Geisel ran into a former classmate, Mike McClintock, who had just been appointed juvenile editor of Vanguard Press. McClintock promptly took him up to his office where they signed a contract. So Dr. Seuss kept on writing. He gave us sixty more wonderfully imaginative, tongue-twisting, colorful, positive books which have enriched and enchanted millions of children and adults around the world.

Don't be afraid to take big steps. You can't cross a chasm in two small jumps.

David Lloyd George

No answer is also an answer.

German Proverb

No one can possibly achieve any real and lasting success or get rich in business by being a conformist.

J. Paul Getty

Trust in dreams, for in them is hidden the gate to eternity.

Kahlil Gibran

Your pain is the breaking of the shell that encloses your understanding.

Kahlil Gibran

Believe those who are seeking the truth; doubt those who find it.

André Gide

One doesn't discover new lands without consenting to lose sight of the shore.

André Gide

When we accept tough jobs as a challenge to our ability and wade into them with joy and enthusiasm, miracles can happen.

Arland Gilbert

Mistakes are a fact of life. It's the response to the error that counts.

Nikki Giovanni

In the darkest night of the year,
When the stars have all gone out,
That courage is better than fear,
That faith is truer than doubt.

Washington Gladden
"Ultima Veritas"

Give to me the benefit of your convictions, if you have any, but keep your doubts to yourself, for I have enough of my own.

Johann Wolfgang von Goethe

Plunge boldly into the thick of life.

Johann Wolfgang von Goethe

The greatest tragedy is suffering the pain without learning the lesson.

Johann Wolfgang von Goethe

The only real obstacle on your path to possibility will always be yourself. Too often we do not see things as they are; we see things as we are.

Stuart Avery Gold

Fight for the privilege to fail.

Willis Goldbeck

William Golding's novel *Lord of the Flies* was rejected by twenty-one publishers before a newly-hired editor at Faber & Faber convinced the publishing house to buy it for £60. Since that time, an estimated 14.5 million copies of the book have been sold. Golding was later knighted by Queen Elizabeth II, and in 1983, he was awarded the Nobel Prize for Literature.

###

The impossible is often the untried.

Jim Goodwin

Life is mostly froth and bubble;
Two things stand like stone:
Kindness in another's trouble
Courage in our own.

Adam Lindsay Gordon
"Finis Exoptatus"

Mediocrity obtains more with application than superiority without it.

Baltasar Gracián
The Art of Worldly Wisdom

Put a grain of boldness into everything you do.

Baltasar Gracián
The Art of Worldly Wisdom

I pretended to be somebody I wanted to be until finally I became that person. Or he became me.

Cary Grant

Failure in a great enterprise is at least a noble fault.

Greek Proverb

One-hundred percent of shots not taken don't go in.

Wayne Gretzky

Believe in yourself, and you will be unstoppable.

Emily Guay

We must overcome the notion that we must be regular... it robs you of the chance to be extraordinary and leads you to the mediocre.

Uta Hagen

Don't be afraid to ask dumb questions. They're more easily handled than dumb mistakes.

William Wister Haines

Nothing is work unless you'd rather be doing something else.

George Halas

He who leaveth nothing to chance will do few things ill, but he will do very few things.

George, Lord Halifax

The only disability in life is a bad attitude.

Scott Hamilton

I don't know who or what put the question. I don't know when it was put. I don't even remember answering. But at some moment, I did answer 'yes' to someone or something, and from that hour, I was certain that existence is meaningful and that, therefore, my life, in self-surrender, had a goal.

Dag Hammarskjöld

We are not permitted to choose the frame of our destiny. But what we put into it is ours.

Dag Hammarskjöld

Don't be afraid your life will end; be afraid that it will never begin.

Grace Hansen

Don't wait until everything is just right. It will never be perfect. There will always be challenges, obstacles and less-than-perfect conditions. So what? Get started now. With each step you take, you will grow stronger and stronger, more and more skilled, more and more self-confident, and more and more successful.

Mark Victor Hansen

The bravest thing you can do when you are not brave is to profess courage and act accordingly.

Corra May White Harris

Success isn't everything, but it makes a man stand straight.

Lillian Hellman

It matters not how strait the gate,
How charged with punishments the scroll,
I am the master of my fate:
I am the captain of my soul.

William Ernest Henley
"Invictus"

The battle is not to the strong alone; it is to the vigilant, the active, the brave.

Patrick Henry

If you obey all the rules, you miss all the fun.

Katharine Hepburn

#

Although **Frank Herbert** had already published multiple articles and one book, and although some publishers liked the trilogy of stories which eventually became *Dune,* twenty-three publishers rejected the manuscript prior to its being accepted by Chilton Book Company, a house better known for its auto-repair manuals than for science fiction. [According to Frank's son Brian, one editor who declined the manuscript told his father that he was probably making the mistake of his lifetime.] Dune went on to win both the Nebula Award for Best Novel and the Hugo Award for Best Science Fiction Novel. It has been made into a movie directed by David Lynch and a Sci Fi Channel TV mini-series. It has also been translated into fourteen languages and, to date, has sold over twelve million copies.

#

There is no merit where there is no trial; and till experience stamps the mark of strength, cowards may pass for heroes, and faith for falsehood.

Aaron Hill

It is not the mountain we conquer, but ourselves.

Edmund Hillary

Cherish your visions and your dreams as they are the children of your soul; the blueprints of your ultimate achievements. When your desires are strong enough, you will appear to possess super-human powers to achieve.

Napoleon Hill

If not now, when?

Hillel the Elder

Strength and courage aren't always measured in medals and victories. They are measured in the struggles they overcome. The strongest people aren't always the people who win, but the people who don't give up when they lose.

Ashley Hodgeson

There can be no real freedom without the freedom to fail.

Eric Hoffer
The Ordeal of Change

They who lack talent expect things to happen without effort. They ascribe failure to a lack of inspiration or ability, or to misfortune, rather than to insufficient application. At the core of every true talent, there is an awareness of the difficulties inherent in any achievement, and the confidence that by persistence and patience something worthwhile will be realized.

Eric Hoffer

Heaven is not reached at a single bound;
But we build the ladder by which we rise
From the lowly earth to the vaulted skies,
And we mount to its summit round by round.

Josiah Gilbert Holland
"Gradatim"

As life is action and passion, it is required of a man that he should share the passion and action of his time, at peril of being judged not to have lived.

Oliver Wendell Holmes, Jr.

I find the great thing in this world is not so much where we stand, as in what direction we are moving. To reach the port of heaven, we must sail sometimes with the wind and sometimes against it -- but we must sail, and not drift, nor lie at anchor.

Oliver Wendell Holmes, Jr.

The secret of my success is that at an early age I discovered I was not God.

Oliver Wendell Holmes, Jr.

A man may fulfill the object of his existence by asking a question he cannot answer and attempting a task he cannot achieve.

Oliver Wendell Holmes, Sr.

Ability is what you're capable of doing. Motivation determines what you do. Attitude determines how well you do it.

Lou Holtz

If you don't make a total commitment to whatever you're doing, then you start looking to bail out the first time the boat starts leaking. It's tough enough getting that boat to shore with everybody rowing, let alone when a guy stands up and starts putting his life jacket on.

Lou Holtz

Without self-discipline, success is impossible, period.

Lou Holtz

Go on with a spirit that fears nothing.

Homer

Carpe diem. (Seize the day.)

Horace

I do not know beneath what sky
Nor on what seas shall be thy fate:
I only know it shall be high,
I only know it shall be great.

Richard Hovey
"Unmanifest Destiny"

Who would not rather founder in the fight
Than not have known the glory of the fray?

Richard Hovey
"Two and Fate"

One-half of knowing what you want is knowing what you must give up before you get it.

Sidney Howard

When a man succeeds, he does it in spite of everybody, and not with the assistance of everybody.

Edgar Watson Howe
Country Town Sayings

Experience is the name every one gives his mistakes.

Elbert Hubbard
The Roycroft Dictionary and Book of Epigrams

Success consists in the climb.

Elbert Hubbard

Be like the bird that, pausing in her flight awhile on boughs too slight, feels them give way beneath her, and yet sings, knowing she hath wings.

Victor Hugo

He dares to be a fool, and that is the first step in the direction of wisdom.

James G. Huneker
Pathos of Distance

Decide what you want.   Decide what you are willing to exchange for it. Establish your priorities and go to work.

H.L. Hunt

Mama exhorted her children at every opportunity to 'jump at de sun.' We might not land on the sun, but at least we would get off the ground.

Zora Neale Hurston
Dust Tracks on a Road

Experience is not what happens to a man; it's what a man does with what happens to him.

Aldous Huxley

Every great advance in natural knowledge has involved the absolute rejection of authority.

T.H. Huxley
Lay Sermons, Addresses and Reviews

So, what do we do? Anything. Something. So long as we just don't sit there. If we screw it up, start over. Try something else. If we wait until we've satisfied all the uncertainties, it may be too late.

Lee Iacocca

The strongest man in the world is he who stands most alone.

Henrik Ibsen
An Enemy of the People

Doubt is the beginning, not the end, of wisdom.

George Iles

Respect the past in the full measure of its desserts, but do not make the mistake of confusing it with the present nor seek in it the ideals of the future.

Jose Incenerios

The greatest test of courage on earth is to bear defeat without losing heart.

Robert G. Ingersoll

Great minds have purposes, little minds have wishes. Little minds are subdued by misfortunes, great minds rise above them.

Washington Irving

Don't fight the problem, decide it.

Walter Isaacson and Evan Thomas
The Wise Men: Six Friends and the World They Made

Once the game is over, the king and pawn go into the same box.

Italian Proverb

One man with courage makes a majority.

Andrew Jackson

I feel that the most important requirement in success is learning to overcome failure. You must learn to tolerate it, but never accept it.

Reggie Jackson

Be not afraid of life. Believe that life is worth living, and your belief will help create the fact.

William James
The Will to Believe

What we truly and earnestly aspire to be, that in some sense we are. The mere aspiration, by changing the frame of mind, for the moment realizes itself.

Anna Jameson

Fall seven times, stand up eight.

Japanese Proverb

I'm a great believer in luck, and I find the harder I work, the more I have of it.

Thomas Jefferson

It is wonderful what may be done if we are always doing.

Thomas Jefferson

Overnight success takes a long time.

Steve Jobs

You don't have to be Magic to be special. You're already special. You're you.

Earvin ("Magic") Johnson

Your world is as big as you make it
I know, for I used to abide
In the narrowest nest in a corner
My wings pressing close to my side

But I sighted the distant horizon
Where the sky-line encircled the sea
And I throbbed with a burning desire
To travel this immensity.

I battered the cordons around me
And cradled my wings on the breeze
Then soared to the uttermost reaches
with rapture, with power, with ease!

Georgia Douglas Johnson
"Your World"

Treat a person as he is, and he will remain as he is. Treat him as he could be, and he will become what he should be.

Jimmy Johnson

If you believe in something, to have the commitment is really more important than having the money.

John H. Johnson

Few things are impossible to diligence and skill. Great works are performed not by strength, but perseverance.

Samuel Johnson

Nothing will ever be attempted, if all possible objections must be first overcome.

Samuel Johnson
Rasselas

We must remember that one determined person can make a significant difference, and that a small group
of determined people can change the course of history.

Sonia Johnson

I never learned a thing from a tournament I won.

Bobby Jones

You can't let each little thing crush you. You have to take every encounter and make yourself larger, rather than allow yourself to be diminished by it.

James Earl Jones

Everyone has talent. What is rare is the courage to follow the talent to the dark place where it leads.

Erica Jong

I went for years not finishing anything. Because, of course, when you finish something you can be judged.

Erica Jong

The trouble is, if you don't risk anything, you risk even more.

Erica Jong

I never intended to become a run-of-the-mill person.

Rep. Barbara Jordan

All great champions, most of whom are optimists, have become great because of... not in spite of... great adversity.

Michael Jordan

If you accept the expectations of others, especially negative ones, then you never will change the outcome. You have to expect things of yourself before you can do them.

Michael Jordan

I've missed more than 9,000 shots in my career. I've lost almost 300 games. Twenty-six times I've been trusted to take the game winning shot ... and missed. I've failed over and over and over again in my life. That is why I succeed.

Michael Jordan

#

Michael Jordan and **Bob Cousy** were both cut from their high school basketball teams (Cousy was cut twice). Jordan went on to become a six-time National Basketball Association (NBA) champion, two-time Olympic gold medalist, fourteen-time All-Star, and is considered by many to be the greatest basketball player of all time. Cousy earned five consecutive NBA titles while with the Boston Celtics, was an all-NBA first-team selection for ten years in a row, held thirteen playoff records, was twice voted most valuable player, and is listed on ESPN's Sports Century top one-hundred athletes list.

#

Mistakes are the portals of discovery.

James Joyce

He said not, 'Thou shalt not be troubled, thou shalt not be tempted, thou shalt not be distressed', but he said, 'Thou shalt not be overcome.'

Julian of Norwich
Revelations of Divine Love

Remember this also, and be well persuaded of its truth: the future is not in the hands of fate, but in ours.

Jules Jusserand

The accomplishment of hopes remains an always-unexpected miracle. But in compensation, the miracle remains forever possible.

Franz Kafka

Problems are only opportunities in work clothes.

Henry J. Kaiser

I believe that any man's finest moment, the greatest fulfillment of all he holds dear, is that moment when he has worked his heart out and lies exhausted on the floor of battle – victorious.

Bela Karolyi

I have found that great people do have in common...an immense belief in themselves and in their mission. They also have great determination as well as an ability to work hard. At the crucial moment of decision, they draw on their accumulated wisdom. Above all, they have integrity.

Yousuf Karsh

The best way to predict the future is to invent it.

Alan Kay

He uttered a triumphant cry: It is accomplished! And it was as though he had said: Everything has begun.

Nikos Kazantzakis
The Last Temptation of Christ

Don't be discouraged by a failure. It can be a positive experience. Failure is, in a sense, the highway to success, inasmuch as every discovery of what is false leads us to seek earnestly after what is true, and every fresh experience points out some form of error which we shall afterwards carefully avoid.

John Keats

Character cannot be developed in ease and quiet. Only through experiences of trial and suffering can the soul be strengthened, vision cleared, ambition inspired, and success achieved.

Helen Keller

To keep our faces toward change and behave like free spirits in the presence of fate is strength undefeatable.

Helen Keller

Your success and happiness lie in you. External conditions are the accidents of life. The great enduring realities are love and service. Joy is the holy fire that keeps our purpose warm and our intelligence aglow. Resolve to keep happy, and your joy and you shall form an invincible host against difficulty.

Helen Keller

A sacred burden is this life ye bear; look on it; lift it; bear it solemnly; fail not for sorrow; falter not for sin; but onward, upward, till the goal ye win.

Fanny Kemble

There are risks and costs to action, but they are far less than the long-range risks of comfortable inaction.

John F. Kennedy

Only those who dare to fail greatly can achieve greatly.

Robert F. Kennedy

Failing is one of the greatest arts in the world. One fails toward success.

Charles Kettering

Our imagination is the only limit to what we can hope to have in the future.

Charles Kettering

If I were to wish for anything, I should not wish for wealth and power, but for the passionate sense of the potential, for the eye, which, ever young and ardent, sees the possible. Pleasure disappoints, possibility never. And what wine is so sparkling, what so fragrant, what so intoxicating, as possibility!

Søren Kierkegaard
Either/Or: A Fragment of Life

Be bold. If you're going to make an error, make a doozy, and don't be afraid to hit the ball.

Billie Jean King

Face your fears; live your passions; be dedicated to your truth.
Billie Jean King

We must accept finite disappointment, but we must never lose infinite hope.
Dr. Martin Luther King, Jr.

Talent is cheaper than table salt. What separates the talented individual from the successful one is a lot of hard work.
Stephen King

You have powers you never dreamed of. You can do things you never thought you could do. There are no limitations in what you can do except the limitations of your own mind.
Darwin P. Kingsley

If you will let me, I will wish you in your future what all men desire – enough work to do, and strength enough to do your work.
Rudyard Kipling

The size of your success is measured by the strength of your desire, the size of your dream, and how you handle disappointment along the way.
Robert Kiyosaki

The will to win is not nearly as important as the will to prepare to win.
Bobby Knight

I do not want to die ... until I have faithfully made the most of my talent and cultivated the seed that was placed in me until the last small twig has grown.
Käthe Kollwitz

God helps those who persevere.
The Koran

Pick battles big enough to matter, small enough to win.
Jonathan Kozol

Failure is not an option.
attributed to Gene Kranz

If what you have done yesterday still looks big to you, you haven't done much today.
Mike Krzyzewski

It takes courage not only to make decisions, but to live with those decisions afterward.

Mike Krzyzewski

I believe that we are solely responsible for our choices, and we have to accept the consequences of every deed, word, and thought throughout our lifetime.

Elisabeth Kűbler-Ross

Surely with us there is a voice within, if only we would listen to it, that tells us so certainly when to go forth into the unknown.

Elisabeth Kűbler-Ross

There are no mistakes, no coincidences. All events are blessings given to us to learn from.

Elisabeth Kűbler-Ross

Hope begins in the dark, the stubborn hope that if you just show up and try to do the right thing, the dawn will come. You wait and watch and work. You don't give up.

Anne Lamott

We are, finally, all wanderers in search of knowledge. Most of us hold the dream of becoming something better than we are, something larger, richer, in some way more important to the world and ourselves. Too often, the way taken is the wrong way, with too much emphasis on what we want to have, rather than what we wish to become.

Louis L'Amour

A journey of a thousand miles must begin with a single step.

Lao Tzu
Tao Te Ching

Hope and fear are inseparable.

La Rochefoucauld
Maxims

The difference between the impossible and the possible lies in a man's determination.

Tommy Lasorda

To the stars through hardships.

Latin Proverb

To be successful, the first thing to do is fall in love with your work.

Sister Mary Lauretta

I've never lost a game in my life. Once in a while, time ran out on me.

Bobby Layne

He who limps is still walking.

Stanislaw J. Lec

Never think that God's delays are God's denials. Hold on. Hold fast. Hold out. Patience is genius.

George-Louis Leclerc, Comte de Buffon

Madeleine L'Engle's most popular work, *A Wrinkle in Time*, was rejected twenty-six times before editors at Farrar, Straus & Giroux accepted it for publication. The book is a masterpiece. It won the John Newbery Medal as the best children's book of 1963; to date, it has sold over eight million copies; and, it is now in its sixty-ninth printing. L'Engle went on to win the ALAN Award for Outstanding Contribution to Adolescent Literature from the National Council of Teachers of English, a whole slew of other awards, and was awarded seventeen honorary doctorates.

Elmore Leonard had written and published multiple short stories and Western novels, several of which were made into Hollywood movies, but his first non-Western novel, *The Big Bounce,* was rejected by eighty-four publishers before being accepted. First Warner Brothers made it into a movie, and then it was accepted by Fawcett Books for publication. Leonard has gone on to write forty additional crime novels and is now considered one of the greats of the genre.

The turning point in the process of growing up is when you discover the core of strength within you survives all hurt.

Max Lerner
The Unfinished Country: a Book of American Symbols

Think wrongly, if you please, but in all cases think for yourself.

Doris Lessing

If you don't have confidence, you'll always find a way not to win.

Carl Lewis

Always bear in mind that your own resolution to succeed is more important than any other one thing.

Abraham Lincoln

Nothing in this world is impossible with a willing heart.

Abraham Lincoln

Whatever you are, be a good one.

Abraham Lincoln

For happiness, one needs security, but joy can spring like a flower even from the cliffs of despair.

Anne Morrow Lindbergh

To have faith where you cannot see; to be willing to work on in the dark; to be conscious of the fact that, so long as you strive for the best, there are better things on the way, this in itself is success.

Katherine Logan

It's easy to have faith in yourself and have discipline when you're a winner, when you're number one. What you've got to have is faith and discipline when you're not yet a winner.

Vince Lombardi

Let me tell you what winning means... you're willing to go longer, work harder, give more than anyone else.

Vince Lombardi

The difference between a successful person and others is not a lack of strength, not a lack of knowledge, but rather a lack of will.

Vince Lombardi

It ain't enough to get the breaks. You gotta know how to use 'em.

Huey P. Long

Look not mournfully into the past. It comes not back again. Wisely improve the present. It is thine. Go forth to meet the shadowy future, without fear.

Henry Wadsworth Longfellow

Not in the clamor of the crowded street,
Not in the shouts and plaudits of the throng,
But in ourselves are triumph and defeat.

Henry Wadsworth Longfellow
"The Poets"

The heights by great men reached and kept
were not attained by sudden flight,
But they, while their companions slept,
were toiling upward in the night.

Henry Wadsworth Longfellow
"The Ladder of St. Augustine"

The lowest ebb is the turn of the tide.

Henry Wadsworth Longfellow
"Loss and Gain"

In great attempts, it is glorious even to fail.

Longinus
On the Sublime

Go with the best you've got.

Al Lopez

Mistakes are part of the dues one pays for a full life.

Sophia Loren

That cause is strong which has, not a multitude, but one strong
man behind it.

James Russell Lowell

Freedom is always and exclusively freedom for the one who
thinks differently.

Rosa Luxemburg

There is no security on this earth; there is only opportunity.

General Douglas MacArthur

Between 1844 and 1858, **Rowland H. Macy** established four
retail stores and a money-lending operation; all of them failed.
His last venture, the founding of the R.H. Macy dry goods store
in Manhattan not only survived but thrived.   The store
eventually became the world's largest.   Through mergers,
acquisitions, innovative sales practices, and of course, the
famous Thanksgiving Day parade, Macy's, Inc. has expanded to
almost 800 sites throughout the United States and Puerto Rico.

###

Reality often astonishes theory.
Ray and Tom Magliozzi: *Car Talk*, **National Public Radio**

It is not impossibilities which fill us with the deepest despair, but possibilities which we have failed to realize.
Robert Mallet
Apostilles ou L'utile et le Futile

You have to believe in happiness, or happiness never comes.
Douglas Malloch
"You Have to Believe"

There is no passion to be found in playing small – in settling for a life that is less than the one you are capable of living.
Nelson Mandela

Risk! Risk anything! Care no more for the opinion of others, for those voices. Do the hardest thing on earth for you. Act for yourself. Face the truth.
Katherine Mansfield

Once all struggle is grasped, miracles are possible.
Mao Tse-Tung

There are powers inside you, if you could discover and use, would make of you everything you ever dreamed or imagined you could become.
Orison Swett Marden

There is no medicine like hope, no incentive so great, and no tonic so powerful as expectation of something tomorrow.
Orison Swett Marden

We lift ourselves by our thought, we climb upon our vision of ourselves. If you want to enlarge your life, you must first enlarge your thought of it and of yourself. Hold the ideal of yourself as you long to be, always, everywhere – your ideal of what you long to attain – the ideal of health, efficiency, success.
Orison Swett Marden

Challenges are what make life interesting; overcoming them is what makes life meaningful.
Joshua J. Marine

###

Bobbie Ann Mason was persistent. She submitted twenty stories to *The New Yorker* during a period of about a year and a half before one was accepted. As she tells it, "The rejection letters were more encouragement than rejection, so I bounded along eagerly, with a new story ready to go almost as soon as one was returned." Mason has gone on to win the PEN/Hemingway Award, the Southern Book Award for Fiction (twice), and her novel *In Country* was made into a Hollywood film co-starring Emily Lloyd and Bruce Willis.

###

My will shall shape my future. Whether I fail or succeed shall be no man's doing but my own. I am the force: I can clear any obstacle before me or I can be lost in the maze. My choice, my responsibility; win or lose, only I hold the key to my destiny.
Elaine Maxwell

You need to claim the events of your life to make yourself yours. When you truly possess all you have been and done, which may take some time, you are fierce with reality.
Florida Scott Maxwell

It is not your environment, it is you – the quality of your mind, the integrity of your soul, and the determination of your will – that will decide your future and shape your life.
Benjamin Elijah Mays, Ph.D.

Caution and cynicism are safe, but soldiers don't want to follow cautious cynics. They follow leaders who believe enough to risk failure and disappointment for a worthy cause.
General Stanley A. McChrystal

Set priorities for your goals. A major part of successful living lies in the ability to put first things first. Indeed, the reason most major goals are not achieved is that we spend our time doing second things first.
Robert J. McKain

Our strength is often composed of the weakness we're damned if we're going to show.
Mignon McLaughlin

My mama taught me that anything worth doing in life should be a little scary.
Terry McMillan

Never doubt that a small group of thoughtful committed citizens can change the world. Indeed, it's the only thing that ever has.

Margaret Mead

If I have changed over the years, I think that my doubts have grown. I hope in the best sense. Mathew Arnold used the phrase 'heroic doubts.' The certainties of the contemporary world appall me, because I think they're based on complacency and a lack of curiosity which lead to rigidity. Nobody has any doubts anymore. If you are in doubt, you listen to another point of view. I've tried to keep that alive.

Gita Mehta

It is better to fail in originality than to succeed in imitation.

Herman Melville

Faith may be defined briefly as an illogical belief in the occurrence of the improbable.

H. L. Mencken
Prejudices

We have what we seek. It is there all the time, and if we give it time, it will make itself known to us.

Thomas Merton

The greatest danger for most of us is not that our aim is too high and we miss it, but that it is too low and we reach it.

Michelangelo

Character consists of what you do on the third and fourth tries.

James A. Michener

When this is over, I'm not going to be the same guy. I'm going to live as if I were a great man.

James A. Michener

One person with a belief is equal to a force of ninety-nine who only have interest.

John Stuart Mill

Every moment is a golden one for him who has the vision to recognize it as such.

Henry Miller

I'd gone through life believing in the strength and competence of others, never in my own. Now, dazzled, I discovered that *my* capacities were real. It was like finding a fortune in the lining of an old coat.

Joan Mills

Yet I argue not
against Heav'n's hand or will, not bate a jot
of heart or hope, but still bear up and steer
right onward.

John Milton
"Sonnet XXII, to Cyriac Skinner"

Reality is something you rise above.

Liza Minnelli

Until you've lost your reputation, you never realize what a burden it was or what freedom really is.

Margaret Mitchell

The greater the obstacle, the more glory in overcoming it.

Molière (Jean-Baptiste Poquelin)

In life, the first thing you must do is decide what you really want. Weigh the costs and the results. Are the results worthy of the costs? Then make up your mind completely and go after your goal with all your might.

Alfred A. Montapert

Pain nourishes courage. You can't be brave if you've had only wonderful things happen to you.

Mary Tyler Moore

There is only one success – to be able to spend your life in your own way.

Christopher Morley
Where the Blues Begin

Bet on yourself. Always.

Elisabeth Moss

Everything is possible, including the impossible and absurd.

Benito Mussolini

A number two pencil and a dream can take you anywhere.

Joyce A. Myers

No great discovery was ever made without a bold guess.

Isaac Newton

What is happiness? The feeling that power is growing, that resistance is overcome.

Friedrich Nietzsche

We can let circumstances rule us, or we can take charge and rule our lives from within.

Earl Nightingale

Life shrinks or expands in proportion to one's courage.

Anaïs Nin

Anything you do that is truly yours is rebellious.

Clare O'Donohue
The Lover's Knot

I don't want to end up simply having visited this world.

Mary Oliver
"When Death Comes"

I take a simple view of living. It is to keep your eyes open and get on with it.

Sir Laurence Olivier

One of life's most painful moments comes when we must admit that we didn't do our homework, that we are not prepared.

Merlin Olsen

Perseverance isn't just the willingness to work hard. It's that, plus the willingness to be stubborn about your own belief in yourself.

Merlin Olsen

At least I tried.

McMurphy (as played by Jack Nicholson)
One Flew over the Cuckoo's Nest

Every day I get up and look through the Forbes list of the richest people in American. If I'm not there, I go to work.

Robert Orben

And though he greatly failed, more greatly dared.

Ovid

Courage conquers all things.

Ovid
Epistulae ex Ponto

Endure and persist; this pain will turn to good by and by.

Ovid
Amores

Judgment comes from experience, and great judgment comes from bad experience.

Senator Bob Packwood

Ain't no man can avoid being born average, but there ain't no man got to be common.

Satchel Paige

The most rewarding things you do in life are often the ones that look like they cannot be done.

Arnold Palmer

The great workmen of history have been men who believed like giants.

Charles Henry Parkhurst
"Walking by Faith"

Just for today, I will be happy. Just for today, I will try to live through this day only, not to tackle my whole life problem at once. I can do things for twelve hours that would appall me if I had to keep them up for a lifetime. Just for today...

Sybyl F. Partridge

The heart has its reasons which reason does not know.

Blaise Pascal

I don't like people who have never fallen or stumbled. Their virtue is lifeless, and it isn't of much value. Life hasn't revealed its beauty to them.

Boris Pasternak

Chance favors only the prepared mind.

Louis Pasteur

Courage is fear holding on a minute longer.

General George S. Patton

The test of success is not what you do when you're on top. Success is how high you bounce when you hit bottom.

General George S. Patton

Any fact facing us is not as important as our attitude toward it, for that determines our success or failure. The way you think about a fact may defeat you before you ever do anything about it. You are overcome by the fact because you think you are.

Norman Vincent Peale

Believe it is possible to solve your problem. Tremendous things happen to the believer. So believe the answer will come. It will.

Norman Vincent Peale

Change your thoughts, and you change your world.

Norman Vincent Peale

Behold, we live through all things – famine, thirst, bereavement, pain; all grief and misery, all woe and sorrow; life inflicts its worst on soul and body – but we cannot die though we be sick and tired and faint and worn. Lo, all things can be borne.

Florence Percy (Elizabeth Chase Akers Allen)
"Endurance"

Dear Lord, please send us blessed dreams,
And let them all come true.

Florence Percy (Elizabeth Chase Akers Allen)
"Blessed Dreams"

If a man will only stick to the thing he loves most he will do it right, and end right.

Maxwell Perkins

\#\#\#

Laurence J. Peter and **Raymond Hull**'s classic business text, *The Peter Principle: Why Things Always Go Wrong* was rejected by thirty publishers before William Morrow & Co. paid the princely sum of $2,500 for the manuscript and deigned to print 10,000. To date, the book has sold more than eight million copies and has been translated into thirty-eight languages.

\#\#\#

The man who makes no mistakes does not usually make anything.

Edward John Phelps

If you have made mistakes, even serious ones, there is always another chance for you. What we call failure is not the falling down, but the staying down.

Mary Pickford

To make no mistakes is not in the power of man, but from their errors and mistakes, the wise and good learn wisdom for the future.

Plutarch

Over the years, **Beatrix Potter** had written many illustrated letters to the children of her former governance, Annie Moore. At Moore's suggestion, Potter used these letters (and her wonderful imagination) to create her first book, *The Tale of Peter Rabbit*. Six publishers failed to see its charm, so the author, believing in herself and her writing, chose to self-publish. After seeing her private edition, Frederick Warne & Co., one of the six companies which had previously rejected the manuscript, reconsidered its prior decision and agreed to produce the book. Potter went on to write twenty-two more illustrated tales (in addition to other works). She also created – literally, by hand - the first Peter Rabbit doll. One hundred ten years later, shoppers still buy her books and dozens of other items based on them: stuffed animals, toys, calendars, money banks, figurines, bedding, china tea-sets, and even organic baby food – all still licensed through Frederick Warne.

There are no secrets to success. It is the result of preparation, hard word, and learning from failure.

General Colin Powell

It is better to live recklessly and dangerously and even disastrously than not to live at all.

Llewelyn Powys
Impassioned Clay

In any contest between power and patience, bet on patience.

W.B. Prescott

In 1954, **Elvis Presley** made his first and only appearance at the Grand Ole Opry. The Opry's manager, Jimmy Denny, fired Elvis Presley after one performance. He told Presley, "You ain't goin' nowhere, son. You ought to go back to drivin' a truck." Elvis, of course, went on to become "The King." It is estimated that his records have sold over one billion copies worldwide.

Patience is invincible.

Pierre-Joseph Proudhon

#

André Gide, French author, winner of the Nobel Prize in Literature, and one of the founders of the literary magazine *Nouvelle Revue Française* rejected *Swann's Way*, the first volume of **Marcel Proust**'s *Remembrance of Things Past*. A year later, he wrote to Proust, "For several days I have been unable to put your book down.... The rejection of this book will remain the most serious mistake ever made by the *NRF,* and since I bear the shame of being very much responsible for it, one of the most stinging and remorseful regrets of my life."

#

Fame for British novelist, **Barbara Pym**, came slowly. Throughout her life, she wrote novels and stories for women's magazines; some were published, but none sold well. [Twenty publishers refused to accept *An Unsuitable Attachment*.] But in 1977, when Pym was sixty-four, *The London Times* asked Britain's best-known writers to name the most underrated novelist of the century: Pym was the only one mentioned twice. Overnight she was a star, and all twelve of her previously-rejected manuscripts were quickly published.

#

The trouble with many plans is that they are based on the way things are now. To be successful, your personal plan must focus on what you want, not what you have.

Nido Qubein

Your present circumstances don't determine where you can go; they merely determine where you start.

Nido Qubein

When you've gotten really good at your job, change it or leave it.

Anna Quindlen

I wanted a perfect ending... Now I've learned, the hard way, that some poems don't rhyme, and some stories don't have a clear beginning, middle and end. Life is about not knowing, having to change, taking the moment and making the best of it, without knowing what's going to happen next.   Delicious ambiguity.

Gilda Radner

Be realistic. Plan for a miracle.

Bhagwan Shree Rajneesh (Osho)

Don't call it uncertainties – call it wonder.   Don't call it insecurity – call it freedom.

Bhagwan Shree Rajneesh (Osho)

All you have to do is look straight and see the road, and when you see it, don't sit looking at it...walk.

Ayn Rand

Instead of thinking about where you are, think about where you want to be.

Diana Rankin

Once you choose hope, anything's possible.

Christopher Reeve

So many of our dreams at first seem impossible, then they seem improbable, and then, when we summon the will, they soon become inevitable.

Christopher Reeve

Failure is not the only punishment for laziness; there is also the success of others.

Jules Renard
The Journal of Jules Renard

Stick with the optimists. It's going to be tough enough even if they're right.

James ("Scotty") Reston

All adventures, especially into new territory, are scary.

Sally Ride

Don't let other people tell you what you want.

Pat Riley

...have patience with everything that remains unsolved in your heart. Try to love the questions themselves, like locked rooms and like books written in a foreign language. Do not now look for the answers. They cannot now be given to you because you could not live them.   It is a question of experiencing everything. At present, you need to live the question. Perhaps you will gradually, without even noticing it, find yourself experiencing the answer, some distant day.

Rainer Maria Rilke

To achieve the impossible, it is precisely the unthinkable that must be thought.

Tom Robbins
Jitterbug Perfume

To believe is to be strong.   Doubt cramps energy.   Belief is power.

Frederick William Robertson

I do not think that there is any other quality so essential to success of any kind as the quality of perseverance.   It overcomes almost everything, even nature.

John D. Rockefeller

Sometime, when the team is up against it – and the breaks are beating the boys – tell them to go out there with all they got and win just one for the Gipper.

Knute Rockne

When the going gets tough, the tough get going.

Knute Rockne

#

Although **Auguste Rodin** had studied at the Petite Ecole des Beaux-Arts, he was denied admission, three times, to the school's affiliated and more prestigious École Nationale Supérieure des Beaux-Arts. Today, his works are in museums and public gardens around the world; there is a museum dedicated solely to his works in Philadelphia; and, he is one of the few sculptors whose name is widely-known outside the visual arts community.

#

The magazines are full of bunk when they write about a fellow winning fame and fortune by working hard and sticking to one job.   All of you know, as well as I do, it was some accident started you off on the right track.

Will Rogers

Even if you are on the right track, you'll get run over if you just sit there.

Will Rogers

To be successful, you don't have to do extraordinary things. Just do ordinary things extraordinarily well.

John Rohn

No one can make you feel inferior without your consent.

Eleanor Roosevelt

The future belongs to those who believe in the beauty of their dreams.

Eleanor Roosevelt

You gain strength, courage and confidence by every experience in which you really stop to look fear in the face. You are able to say to yourself, 'I have lived through this horror. I can take the next thing that comes along.' You must do the thing you think you cannot do.

Eleanor Roosevelt

The only limit to our realization of tomorrow will be our doubts of today.

Franklin Delano Roosevelt

The only thing we have to fear is fear itself.

Franklin Delano Roosevelt

Courage is not having the strength to go on; it is going on when you don't have the strength. Industry and determination can do anything that genius and advantage can do, and many things that they cannot.

Theodore Roosevelt

Far and away the best prize that life offers is the chance to work hard at work worth doing.

Theodore Roosevelt

It is not the critic who counts, not the man who points out how the strong man stumbled, or where the doer of deeds could have done better. The credit belongs to the man who is actually in the arena, whose face is marred by dust and sweat and blood, who strives valiantly, who errs and comes short again and again, who knows the great enthusiasms, the great devotions, and spends himself in a worthy cause, who at best knows achievement and who at the worst if he fails at least fails while daring greatly so that his place shall never be with those cold and timid souls who know neither victory nor defeat.

Theodore Roosevelt

Mankind has advanced in the footsteps of men and women of unshakable faith. Many of the great ones... have set stars in the heavens to light others through the night.

Olga Rosmanith

It takes great effort to become effortless at anything.

Geneen Roth
Women Food and God: An Unexpected Path to Almost Everything

Patience is bitter, but its fruit is sweet.

Jean-Jacques Rousseau
Emile, or On Education

The follies which a man regrets the most in his life are those which he didn't commit when he had the opportunity.

Helen Rowland

J.K. Rowling's *Harry Potter and the Philosopher's Stone* was rejected by one literary agency [She has said that when she sent off the first three chapters, they were "... returned... so fast they must have been sent back the same day they arrived"] and twelve publishing houses before being accepted for publication. Although Bloomsbury agreed to publish the book, its editor, Barry Cunningham, says that he advised Rowling to get a day job, since she had little chance of making money in children's books. Her seven books about the wizard have been translated into over seventy languages (including ancient Greek) and have sold over 400 million copies worldwide. Rowling is believed to be the first novelist ever to become a billionaire as a result of her writing.

He's not very fast, but maybe Elizabeth Taylor can't sing.

Darrell Royal

Per ardua ad astra (Through endeavor to the stars)

Motto of the (British) Royal Air Force

I don't believe I have special talents. I have persistence. After the first failure, second failure, third failure, I kept trying.

Carlo Rubbia

However confused the scene of our life appears, however torn we may be who now do face that scene, it can be faced, and we can go on to be whole.

Muriel Rukeyser

If you are not criticized, you may not be doing much.

Donald Rumsfeld

Aim well. Err honestly.

Ben Rush

Do not fear to be eccentric in opinion, for every opinion now accepted was once eccentric.

Bertrand Russell

To conquer fear is the beginning of wisdom, in the pursuit of truth as in the endeavour after a worthy manner of life.

Bertrand Russell

Flops are a part of life's menu, and I've never been a girl to miss out on any of the courses.

Rosalind Russell

Pray to God, but keep rowing to shore.

Russian Proverb

The future belongs to him who knows how to wait.

Russian Proverb

Baseball legend **Babe Ruth** is, of course, famous for his slugging. He hit 714 home runs in his career with a lifetime batting average of .342. But it is worth remembering that he also struck out 1,330 times. His philosophy was, "Every strike brings me closer to the next home run."

There is always a multitude of reasons both in favour of doing a thing and against doing it. The art of debate lies in presenting them; the art of life lies in neglecting ninety-nine hundredths of them.

Mark Rutherford
More Pages from a Journal

Somewhere, something incredible is waiting to be known.

Carl Sagan

Every man is the architect of his own fortune.

Sallust (Gaius Sallustius Crispus)

Work is not man's punishment. It is his reward and his strength and his pleasure.

George Sand

Nothing happens unless first a dream.

Carl Sandburg
"Washington Monument by Night"

It is wisdom to believe the heart.

George Santayana

Progress, far from consisting in change, depends on retentiveness. Those who cannot remember the past are condemned to repeat it.

George Santayana

We must not allow other people's limited perceptions to define us.

Virginia Satir

The future is not a result of choices among alternative paths offered by the present, but a place that is created – created first in the mind and will, created next in activity. The future is not some place we are going to, but one we are creating. The paths are not to be found, but made, and the activity of making them changes both the maker and the destination.

John Schaar

Victory isn't defined by wins or losses. It is defined by effort. If you can truthfully say, 'I did the best I could, I gave everything I had,' then you're a winner.

Wolfgang Schadler

All truth passes through three stages: First, it is ridiculed. Second, it is violently opposed. Third, it is accepted as being self-evident.

Arthur Schopenhauer

Again and again, the impossible problem is solved when we see that the problem is only a tough
decision waiting to be made.

Robert H. Schuller

What would you attempt if you knew you could not fail?
Robert H. Schuller

###

In high school, **Charles Schulz** flunked Latin, English, algebra and physics, and all the cartoons he drew for his high school yearbook were rejected. But Schulz went on to draw Charlie Brown and his crew of friends for nearly fifty years. Eventually "Peanuts" reached readers in seventy-five countries, 2,600 papers, and twenty-one languages, and made its creator very, very rich. The strips, merchandise and product endorsements brought in $1.1 billion a year, and Schulz was said to have earned about $30 million to $40 million annually.

###

Only she who attempts the absurd can achieve the impossible.
Sharon Schuster

Hard work is the best investment a man can make.
Charles M. Schwab
"Ten Commandments of Success"

The will to do, the soul to dare.
Walter Scott
The Lady of the Lake

To have your back to a cliff, that's the best way to accomplish something. Never have anything to fall back on.
Jerry Seinfeld

Luck is what happens when preparation meets opportunity.
Seneca

Sometimes even to live is an act of courage.
Seneca
"Letters to Lucilius"

Put your ear down close to your soul and listen hard.
Anne Sexton

Our doubts are traitors,
And make us lose the good we oft might win
By fearing to attempt.

William Shakespeare
Measure for Measure

Presume not that I am the thing I was.

William Shakespeare
Henry IV

To thine own self be true.

William Shakespeare
Hamlet

If you take too long in deciding what to do with your life, you'll find you've done it.

George Bernard Shaw

Imagination is the beginning of creation. You imagine what you desire, you will what you imagine, and at last, you create what you will.

George Bernard Shaw

You see things, and you say, 'Why?' But I dream things that never were, and I say, 'Why not?'

George Bernard Shaw

I finished my first book seventy-six years ago. I offered it to every publisher on the English-speaking earth I had ever heard of. Their refusals were unanimous, and it did not get into print until, fifty years later.

George Bernard Shaw

A ship in harbor is safe, but that is not what ships are built for.

John A. Shedd

Opportunities are seldom labeled.

John A. Shedd

Happiness has something to do with struggling and enduring and accomplishing.

George Sheehan

To suffer woes which Hope thinks infinite;
To forgive wrongs darker than death or night;
To defy Power, which seems omnipotent;
To love, and bear; to hope till Hope creates
From its own wreck the thing it contemplates;
Neither to change nor falter, nor repent;
This, like thy glory, Titan, is to be
Good, great and joyous, beautiful and free;
This is alone Life, Joy, Empire, and Victory.

Percy Bysshe Shelley
Prometheus Unbound

I would define true courage to be a perfect sensibility of the measure of danger, and a mental willingness to endure it.

William Tecumseh Sherman

Success is not the result of spontaneous combustion. You must first set yourself on fire.

Fred Shero

In great moments, life seems neither right nor wrong, but something greater: it seems inevitable.

Margaret Sherwood

Every great work, every great accomplishment, has been brought into manifestation through holding to the vision, and often just before the big achievement, comes apparent failure and discouragement.

Florence Scovel Shinn

Who shoots at the midday sun, though he be sure he shall never hit the mark, yet as sure he is, he shall shoot higher than he who aims at a bush.

Philip Sidney

There are no shortcuts to any place worth going.

Beverly Sills

There is something to be said for keeping at a thing, isn't there?

Frank Sinatra

And now the matchless deed's achieved,
Determin'd, dar'd, and done.

Christopher Smart

Hope is the companion of power and mother of success, for who so hopes strongly has within him the gift of miracles.

Samuel Smiles

It is a mistake to suppose that men succeed through success; they much oftener succeed through failures. Precept, study, advice, and example could nave have taught them so well as failure has done.

Samuel Smiles

What to do with a mistake – recognize it, admit it, learn from it, forget it.

Dean Smith

The test of a vocation is the love of the drudgery it involves.

Logan Pearsall Smith
Afterthoughts

While everyone else is sleeping, I'm working.

Will Smith

Swing hard, in case they throw the ball where you're swinging.

Duke Snider

They were filled with the fearlessness of those who have lost everything, the fearlessness which is not easy to come by, but which endures.

Alexander Isayevich Solzhenitsyn
The First Circle

Welcome every problem as an opportunity. Each moment is the great challenge, the best thing that ever happened to you. The more difficult the problem, the greater the challenge in working it out.

Grace Speare

Let me win. But if I cannot win, let me be brave in the attempt.

Special Olympics Oath

Be bold, be bold, and everywhere be bold.

Edmund Spenser
The Faerie Queen

By perseverance the snail reached the ark.

Charles Spurgeon

If I had to live my life over again, I'd dare to make more mistakes next time.

Nadine Stair

There can be no happiness if the things we believe in are different from the things we do.

Freya Madeline Stark

Reach high, for the stars lie hidden in your soul. Dream deep, for every dream precedes the goal.

Pamela Vaull Starr

Let me listen to me and not to them.

Gertrude Stein

Most ball games are lost, not won.

Casey Stengel

After the final no there comes a yes
And on that yes the future world depends.
No was the night. Yes is this present sun.

Wallace Stevens
"The Well-Dressed Man with a Beard"

...we are now on the eve of great decisions, not easy decisions.

Adlai Stevenson

Everyone who achieves success in a great venture, solved each problem as they came to it. They helped themselves. And they were helped by powers known and unknown to them at the time they set out on their voyage. They kept going regardless of the obstacles they met.

Clement Stone

###

Budding playwright, **Irving Stone,** was prolific but not successful: in a single year he churned out seventeen plays, none of which sold. Over a three-year period, fifteen? sixteen? seventeen? * publishers rejected his first manuscript *Lust for Life*. Someone finally recognized his talent, and the book was published. Stone went on to write about such historical figures as Michelangelo, Sigmund Freud, Mary Todd and Abraham Lincoln, and Charles Darwin. His books have sold tens of millions of copies; they have been translated into more than seventy languages; and, four have been made into movies.

*Sources vary – maybe Stone lost count after so many

###

Live by what you trust, not by what you fear.

Emery Styron

Not many people are willing to give failure a second opportunity. They fail once, and it is all over. The bitter pill of failure is often more than most people can handle. If you are willing to accept failure and learn from it, if you are willing to consider failure as a blessing in disguise and bounce back, you have got the essential of harnessing one of the most powerful success forces.

Joseph Sugarman

What we prepare for is what we shall get.

William Graham Sumner

Define success on your own terms, achieve it by your own rules, and build a life you're proud to live.

Anne Sweeney

May you live all the days of your life.

Jonathan Swift
Polite Conversation

Vision is the art of seeing things invisible.

Jonathan Swift

I cannot give you the formula for success, but I can give you the formula for failure, which is: try to please everybody.

Herbert Bayard Swope

Anyone can steer the ship when the sea is calm.

Publilius Syrus
Sententiæ

Discovery consists of seeing what everybody has seen and thinking what nobody has thought.

Albert Szent-Gyorgyi

Success is getting up one more time.

Harold Taylor

A sailor without a destination cannot hope for a favorable wind.

Leon Tec, M.D.

'Are you not,' a Rugby master had asked him in discussing one of his essays, 'a little out of your depth here?' 'Perhaps, Sir,' was the confident reply, 'but I can swim.'

William Temple

For man is man and master of his fate.

Alfred, Lord Tennyson
"Idylls of the King: Song from the Marriage of Geraint"

Is the goal so far away?
Far, how far no tongue can say,
Let us dream our dream to-day.

Alfred, Lord Tennyson

To strive, to seek, to find, and not to yield.

Alfred, Lord Tennyson
"Ulysses"

Fortune favors the brave.

attributed to Terence (Publius Terentius Afer)

I believe because it is impossible.

Tertullian (Quintus Septimius Florens Tertullianus)

The night is long and pain weighs heavily,
But God will hold His word above despair:
Look to the East, where up the lucid sky
The morning climbs; The day shall yet be fair.

Celia Laighton Thaxter
"Faith"

If a man does not keep pace with his companions, perhaps it is because he hears a different drummer. Let him step to the music which he hears, however measured or far away.

Henry David Thoreau

If one advances confidently in the direction of his dreams and endeavors to live the life which he has imagined, he will meet with a success unexpected in common hours.

Henry David Thoreau

Things do not change; we change.

Henry David Thoreau

The bravest are surely those who have the clearest vision of what is before them, glory and danger alike, and yet notwithstanding, go out to meet it.

Thucydides

It is better to ask some of the questions than to know all the answers.

James Thurber
"The Scotty Who Knew Too Much"

Change is not merely necessary to life, it is life.

Alvin Toffler

Accept each moment as if you had chosen it. That frees you of all negativity. Then take action and do what you have to do.

Eckhart Tolle

It's dogged as does it. It ain't thinking about it.

Anthony Trollope
Last Chronicle of Barset

...never think that you're not good enough yourself. A man should never think that. My belief is that in life people will take you very much at your own reckoning.

Anthony Trollope

The buck stops here.

Harry S. Truman

The next best thing to winning is losing! At least you've been in the race.

Nellie Hershey Tullis

All you need in this life is ignorance and confidence, and then success is sure.

Mark Twain (Samuel Langhorne Clemens)

Courage is resistance to fear, mastery of fear, not absence of fear.

Mark Twain (Samuel Langhorne Clemens)

It isn't the size of the dog in the fight that counts; it's the size of the fight in the dog.

attributed to Mark Twain
(Samuel Langhorne Clemens)

I learned... that inspiration does not come like a bolt, nor is it kinetic, energetic striving, but it comes into us slowly and quietly and all the time, though we must regularly and every day give it a little chance to start flowing, prime it with a little solitude and idleness.

Brenda Ueland

Vision to see. Faith to believe. Courage to do.
Plaque outside Union Station, Los Angeles, California

God, though this life is but a wraith,
Although we know not what we use,
Although we grope with little faith,
Give me the heart to fight — and lose.

**Louis Untermeyer
"Prayer"**

Straight from a mighty bow this truth is driven: They fail, and they alone, who have not striven.

**Clarence Urmy
"The Arrow"**

Heaven is blest with perfect rest, but the blessing of Earth is toil.

**Henry Van Dyke
"The Toiling of Felix"**

Use what talents you possess – the woods would be very silent if no birds sang there except those that sang best.

Henry Van Dyke

We are not interested in the possibilities of defeat.

Queen Victoria

For they conquer who believe they can.

Virgil

If I cannot prevail upon heaven, I shall move hell.

Virgil

Faith consists in believing when it is beyond the power of reason to believe. It is not enough that a thing be possible for it to be believed.

Voltaire (François-Marie Arouet)

Don't be afraid of your own strength.

Diane Von Furstenberg

Whatever you would do, begin it. Boldness has courage, genius, and magic in it.

Johann Wolfgang von Goethe

Our happiness or unhappiness depends far more on the way we meet the events of life than on the nature of those events themselves.

Wilhelm von Humboldt

In actual life, every great enterprise begins with and takes its first forward step in faith.

August Wilhelm von Schlegel

The reason most people never reach their goals is that they don't define them, or ever seriously consider them as believable or achievable. Winners can tell you where they are going, what they plan to do along the way, and who will be sharing the adventure with them.

Denis Waitley

I had to pick myself up and get on with it, do it all over again, only even better this time.

Sam Walton

I have learned that success is to be measured not so much by the position that one has reached in life as by the obstacles which he has overcome.

Booker T. Washington
Up from Slavery

If we are wise, let us prepare for the worst.

George Washington

Would you like me to give you a formula for success? It's quite simple, really. Double your rate of failure. You are thinking of failure as the enemy of success. But it isn't at all. You can be discouraged by failure – or you can learn from it. So go ahead and make mistakes. Make all you can. Because, remember, that's where you will find success.

Thomas J. Watson

Saddle your dreams afore you ride 'em.

Mary Webb

Miracles sometimes occur, but one has to work terribly hard for them.

Chaim Weizmann

All serious daring starts from within.

Eudora Welty

It doesn't matter if it takes a long time getting there; the point is to have a destination.

Eudora Welty

Faith, mighty faith, the promise sees,
And looks to that alone;
Laughs at impossibilities,
And cries, It shall be done!

Charles Wesley
"Hymn #360"

You can't get much done in life if you only work on the days when you feel good.

Jerry West

The crime is not to avoid failure. The crime is not to give triumph a chance.

Huw Wheldon

When you make a mistake, don't look back at it long. Take the reason of the thing into your mind and then look forward. Mistakes are lessons of wisdom. The past cannot be changed. The future is yet in your power.

Hugh White

Change has a considerable psychological impact on the human mind. To the fearful, it is threatening because it means that things may get worse. To the hopeful, it is encouraging because things may get better. To the confident, it is inspiring because the challenge exists to make thing better.

King Whitney, Jr.

Like the winds of the sea are the ways of fate;
As the voyage along thru life;
'Tis the will of the soul
That decides its goal,
And not the calm or the strife.

Ella Wheeler Wilcox

You can't steal second base and keep one foot on first.

Frederick B. Wilcox

Experience is the name every one gives to their mistakes.

Oscar Wilde

Nowadays most people die of a sort of creeping common sense, and discover when it is too late that the only things one never regrets are one's mistakes.

Oscar Wilde

You have to have a dream so you can get up in the morning.

Billy Wilder

Hope, like faith, is nothing if it is not courageous. It is nothing if it is not ridiculous.

Thornton Wilder

If you fail the first time, that's just a chance to start over again.

Lenny Wilkens

Climb high. Climb far. Your goal the sky. Your aim the star.

Inscription on Williams College gates, Williamstown, Massachusetts.

It doesn't happen all at once. You become. It takes a long time.

Margery Williams

Courage is a moral quality: it is not a chance gift of nature like an aptitude for games. It is a cold choice between two alternatives, the fixed resolve not to quit: an act of renunciation which must be made, not once, but many times by the power of will

Charles McMoran Wilson, Lord Moran

We grow great by dreams. All big men are dreamers. They see things in the soft haze of a spring day or in the red fire of a long winter's evening. Some of us let these great dreams die, but others nourish and protect them; nurse them through the bad days till they bring them to the sunshine and light which comes always to those who sincerely hope that their dreams will come true.

Woodrow Wilson

I believe that one of life's greatest risks is never daring to risk.

Oprah Winfrey

Right now, you are one choice away from a new beginning -- one that leads you toward becoming the fullest human being you can be.

Oprah Winfrey

... there have been no failures in my life... There have been some tremendous lessons.

Oprah Winfrey

If a man has a talent and can't use it, he has failed. If he has a talent and uses only half of it, he has partly failed. If he has a talent and learns somehow to use the whole of it, he has gloriously succeeded, and won a satisfaction and a triumph few men ever know.

Thomas Wolfe

Be more concerned with your character than your reputation, because your character is what you really are, while your reputation is merely what others think you are.

John Wooden

Don't let what you cannot do interfere with what you can do.

John Wooden

It's what you learn after you know it all that counts.

John Wooden

It takes great courage to break with one's past history and stand alone.

Marion Woodman
Addiction to Perfection: The Still Unravished Bride

Out of the strain of the Doing,
Into the peace of the Done.

Julia Louise Woodruff

The truth is more important than the facts.

Frank Lloyd Wright

The future belongs to those who prepare for it today.

Malcolm X

In dreams begins responsibility.

William Butler Yeats

What you lack in talent can be made up with desire, hustle, and giving 110 percent all the time.

Don Zimmer

No matter how full a reservoir of maxims one may possess, and no matter how good one's sentiments may be, if one has not taken advantage of every concrete opportunity to act, one's character may retain entirely unaffected for the better. With mere good intentions, hell is proverbially paved.

William James

Bibliography

I started collecting quotes when I was in college - long, long before I ever thought I would put together this book – so over the years, I didn't keep careful citation records. Some of the quotes within this volume came from the following sources, but for the most part, they are serendipitous discoveries with no citations available.

The following were used primarily to verify facts within the boxed blurbs scattered throughout the text.

#

Andrews, Robert. *Famous Lines: The Columbia Dictionary of Familiar Quotations*. New York: Columbia University Press, 1997.

Bell, Janet Cheatham. *Till Victory Is Won: Famous Black Quotations from the NAACP*. New York: Washington Square Press, Published by Pocket Books, 2002.

Benson, Michael. *Winning Words: Classic Quotes from the World of Sports*. New York: Taylor Trade Publishing, 2008.

Bernard, André. *Rotten Rejections: A Literary Companion*. Wainscott, New York: Pushcart Press, 1990.

Bryant, Howard. *The Last Hero: A Life of Henry Aaron*. New York: Pantheon Books, 2010.

California Governor and First Lady's Conference on Women. *We Empower: Inspirational Wisdom for Women*. New York: Hyperion, 2008.

Carruth, Gorton and Eugene Ehrlich. *The Harper Book of American Quotations*. New York: Harper & Row, Publishers, 1988.

Champigneulle, Bernard. *Rodin*. London: Thames and Hudson, Ltd, 1967.

Cummings, E. E. *No Thanks*. New York: Liveright, 1978.

Fulghum, Robert. *Words I Wish I Wrote: A Collection of Writing That Inspired My Ideas*. New York: Cliff Street Books, an Imprint of HarperCollins Publishers, 1997.

Grippo, Robert M. *Macy's: The Store. The Star. The Story.* Garden City Park, New York: Square One Publishers, 2009.

Gross, John. *The Oxford Book of Aphorisms.* New York: Oxford University Press, 1983.

Herbert, Brian. *Dreamer of Dune: The Biography of Frank Herbert.* New York: A Tom Doherty Associates Book, 2003.

Hughey, Billy and Janice. *A Rainbow of Hope: 777 Inspirational Quotes Plus Selected Scriptures.* El Reno, Oklahoma: Rainbow Studios, Inc. 1992.

Karon, Jan. *A Continual Feast: Words of Comfort and Celebration Collected by Father Tim.* New York: Viking, Published by Penguin Group, 2005.

Karon, Jan. *Patches of Godlight: Father Tim's Favorite Quotes.* New York: Viking, Published by Penguin Group, 2001.

Kennedy, Richard S. *Dreams in the Mirror: A Biography of E. E. Cummings.* New York: Liveright Publishing Corporation, 1980.

Maher, Suzanne. *Eternity: Healing Quotations and Thoughts in Times of Sadness and Loss.* Bellingen, New South Wales, Australia: Affirmations Australia Pty. Ltd, 2006.

Mead, Frank S. *12,000 Inspirational Quotations: A Treasury of Spiritual Insights and Practical Wisdom.* Springfield, Massachusetts: Federal Street Press, A Division of Merriam-Webster, Incorporated, 2000.

Mencken, H.L. *A New Dictionary of Quotations on Historical Principles from Ancient & Modern Sources.* New York: Alfred A. Knopf, Inc, 1985.

Macmillan Publishing Company. *The Macmillan Dictionary of Quotations.* New York: Macmillan Publishing Company, 1989.

Myers, Eric. *Uncle Mame: The Life of Patrick Dennis.* New York: St. Martin's Press, 2000.

Prochnow, Herbert V. and Herbert V. Prochnow, Jr. *The Public Speaker's Treasure Chest: A Compendium of Source Material to Make Your Speech Sparkle.* New York: Harper & Row Publishers, 1942.

Reisler, Jim. *Babe Ruth: Launching the Legend*. New York: McGraw-Hill, 2004.

Thomsett, Michael C. and Linda Rose Thomsett. *A Speaker's Treasury of Quotations: Maxims, Witticisms and Quips for Speeches and Presentations*. Jefferson, North Carolina: McFarland & Company, Inc., Publishers, 2009.

Warner, Carolyn. *The Last Word: A Treasury of Women's Quotes*. Englewood Cliffs, New Jersey: Prentice Hall, 1992.

Wilhelm, Hans. *The Book of Courage*. Hauppauge, New York: Barron's Educational Series, Inc., 2006.

About the Author

Mary Boland is a writer and quilter living in small town Maryland. She is a freelance editor, writes reviews on quilting books, and in her usual interested-in-everything style, she is currently working on a manuscript of gluten-free cookie recipes and concurrently working on a manuscript about Congressional voting rights in the District of Columbia.

Mary can be reached at QQandC@hotmail.com. Her book reviews and quilts can be seen at www.qqandc.com.

www.ingramcontent.com/pod-product-compliance
Lightning Source LLC
Chambersburg PA
CBHW070557290526
45790CB00002B/722